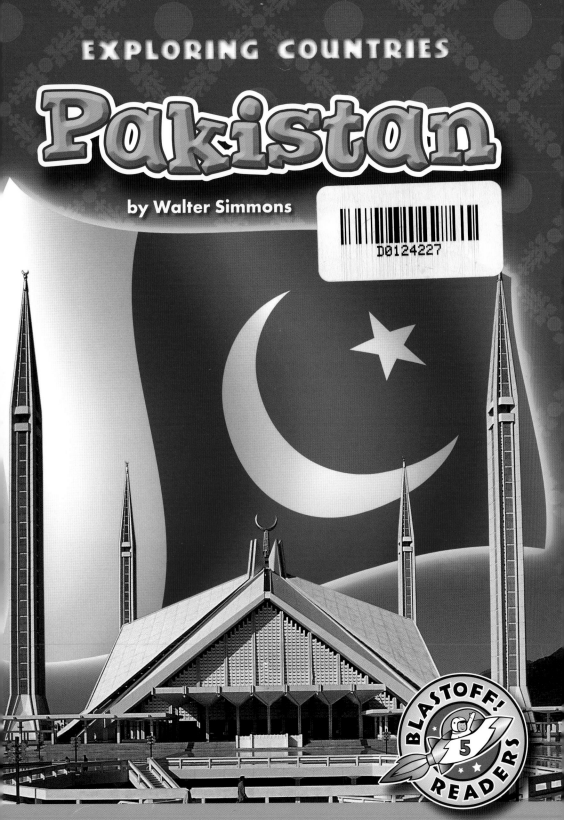

EXPLORING COUNTRIES

Pakistan

by Walter Simmons

D0124227

BELLWETHER MEDIA • MINNEAPOLIS, MN

BLASTOFF!
5
READERS

Note to Librarians, Teachers, and Parents:

Blastoff! Readers are carefully developed by literacy experts and combine standards-based content with developmentally appropriate text.

Level 1 provides the most support through repetition of high-frequency words, light text, predictable sentence patterns, and strong visual support.

Level 2 offers early readers a bit more challenge through varied simple sentences, increased text load, and less repetition of high-frequency words.

Level 3 advances early-fluent readers toward fluency through increased text and concept load, less reliance on visuals, longer sentences, and more literary language.

Level 4 builds reading stamina by providing more text per page, increased use of punctuation, greater variation in sentence patterns, and increasingly challenging vocabulary.

Level 5 encourages children to move from "learning to read" to "reading to learn" by providing even more text, varied writing styles, and less familiar topics.

Whichever book is right for your reader, Blastoff! Readers are the perfect books to build confidence and encourage a love of reading that will last a lifetime!

This edition first published in 2011 by Bellwether Media, Inc.

No part of this publication may be reproduced in whole or in part without written permission of the publisher. For information regarding permission, write to Bellwether Media, Inc., Attention: Permissions Department, 5357 Penn Avenue South, Minneapolis, MN 55419.

Library of Congress Cataloging-in-Publication Data
Simmons, Walter (Walter G.)
Pakistan / by Walter Simmons.
    p. cm. – (Exploring countries) (Blastoff! readers)
Includes bibliographical references and index.
Summary: "Developed by literacy experts for students in grades three through seven, this book introduces young readers to the geography and culture of Pakistan"–Provided by publisher.
ISBN 978-1-60014-593-3 (hardcover : alk. paper)
1. Pakistan–Juvenile literature. I. Title.
DS376.9.S54 2011
954.91–dc22   2010040804

Printed in the United States of America, North Mankato, MN.

010111   1176

Contents

Afghanistan

Islamabad ★

Did you know?

Pakistan was part of India until 1947. In that year, the country split into two parts, one on each side of India. After 1971, East Pakistan became Bangladesh, and West Pakistan became Pakistan.

Pakistan

Iran

Arabian Sea

China

Kashmir

India

Pakistan is a country in southern Asia that covers 307,374 square miles (796,095 square kilometers). It borders Iran and Afghanistan to the west. China is Pakistan's northern neighbor, and India lies to the east. The Arabian Sea washes onto the southern coast of Pakistan. The country's capital is Islamabad.

In the northeast is a region known as **Kashmir**. Kashmir's border has been disputed for many years. Pakistan, China, and India all claim parts of the region. This has brought India and Pakistan to war several times.

K2

! fun fact

K2 is the second-highest mountain in the world. Pakistanis never gave it a name because it is far from any town or village. It was named by Thomas Montgomerie, a British man who labeled the mountain "K2" on his map.

Pakistan has tall mountains, large deserts, and wide, flat river valleys. The Himalayan Mountains rise in northern Pakistan. They have some of the highest peaks in the world. Near the border with China is Pakistan's highest point, K2. This mountain rises to 28,251 feet (8,611 meters).

The Thar Desert stretches along the border with India. Sand **dunes** cover this flat landscape. In southwestern Pakistan, there is a hot, dry region called Balochistan. To the north lie the Spin Ghar Mountains. The Khyber Pass is a famous route through these mountains. The pass links Pakistan and Afghanistan.

The Indus River

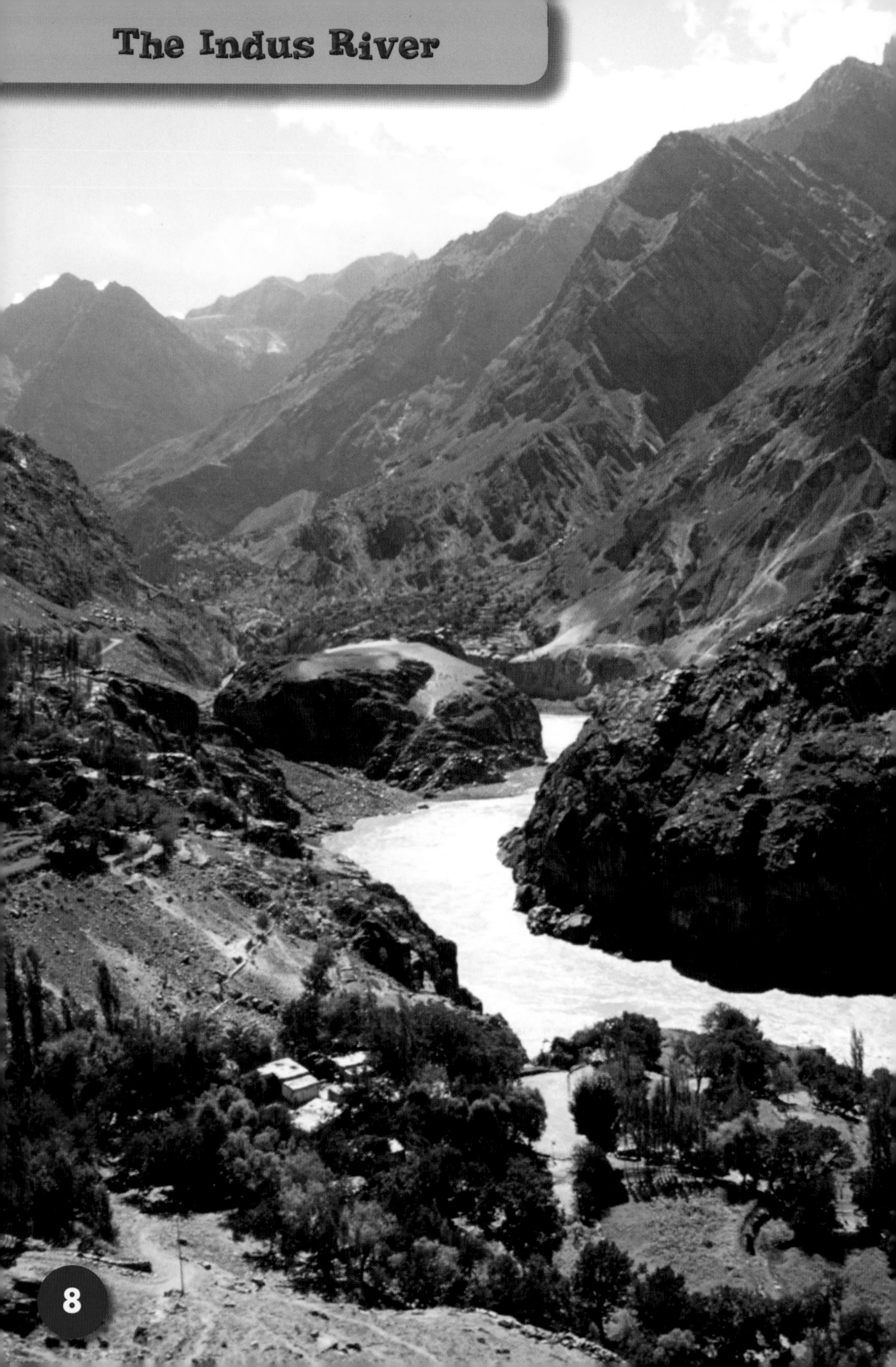

The Indus River flows through the center of Pakistan. Cities and villages crowd the plains along the Indus. The river runs for 1,800 miles (2,900 kilometers) and empties into the Arabian Sea.

The Indus has been a center of civilization for a long time. **Archaeologists** have discovered many ancient cities in the river's valley. Farmers have used the Indus and its **tributaries** to water crops for thousands of years. In the late summer, the river often overflows. This flooding can sweep away crops and livestock. It can cover nearly half of Pakistan's towns with water!

fun fact

The Indus is a wide, powerful river. It carries twice as much water as the Nile, the longest river in the world!

cobra

Indian rhinoceros

markhor

fun fact

The mountains and hills of Pakistan are home to the markhor, the country's national animal.

Pakistan is home to a variety of wildlife. Many rare animals live in the country's mountains, including snow leopards and Sindh ibexes. Marco Polo sheep, named after the famous explorer, also share this **habitat**.

snow leopard

Did you know?
The Indus River is home to the rare Indus dolphin. These dolphins are nearly blind, and only around 1,000 remain.

In the Indus River Valley, foxes and wild boars are plentiful. Dangerous cobras and kraits slither across the plains. The **wetlands** of northern Pakistan are home to the Indian rhinoceros. This animal can weigh up to 6,600 pounds (3,000 kilograms) and run at speeds up to 34 miles (55 kilometers) per hour!

More than 184 million people live in Pakistan.
The nation includes several different groups of people.
Punjabis live in the east. The southern province of
Sindh is home to the Sindhis, and the Baloch people
live in Balochistan. Muhajirs live throughout Pakistan.
These people are **refugees** who came from India
when India and Pakistan separated in 1947.

Urdu and English are the official languages of Pakistan.
Urdu is similar to Hindi, the main language spoken in India.
Many Pakistanis learn English in school, and Pakistan has
English books, newspapers, and television stations.

Did you know?

More people live in Pakistan than in Russia, a country that is over 20 times larger than Pakistan.

Speak Urdu!

Urdu is written in script. However, Urdu words can be
written in English to help you read them out loud.

English	Urdu	How to say it
hello	salam	sa-LAAM
good-bye	kh'udaa haafiz	khoo-dah HAH-fizz
yes	haan	haa
no	nahiin	nah-HEE
please	kijiya	kee-GEE-ya
thank you	shukriya	shoo-KREE-yah
friend	dost	doost

Life in Pakistan's cities differs from life in the countryside. In the cities, most people live in apartments. They use public buses or walk to get around town. The streets are crowded with traffic, people, and vendors who sell food and goods. The roads are too small to hold all the people who need to use them.

In the countryside, people live in homes made of clay or stone. These materials help the houses stay cool. Farmers rise early in the morning to work. They often share a vehicle with neighbors when they need to travel long distances. Many people are moving from the countryside to the cities in search of work.

Where People Live in Pakistan

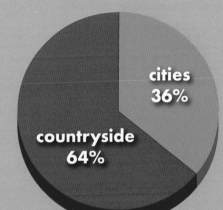

cities
36%

countryside
64%

Did you know?

In Pakistan, people wear long and loose clothing to stay cool. Men and women both wear a long shirt known as a *shalwar kameez*.

In Pakistan, schools teach boys and girls separately. Elementary school lasts from grades one to five. Middle school covers grades six to eight. At this level, students study Urdu, math, science, art, and the history and teachings of Islam. Some also take courses in English.

After middle school, students attend a different school for grades nine and ten. Beyond that, they can choose to take two more years of school to prepare them for university. Students who go to university can study for many different careers.

fun fact

Allama Iqbal Open University in Islamabad has over 1.8 million students!

cricket

Pakistanis enjoy many sports and activities. Field hockey and cricket are two of the most popular sports. Both have national teams that compete against other countries. Badminton and **squash** are also common sports in Pakistan. Thousands of young badminton and squash players hope to make it to the **Olympics**.

Pakistanis also like to relax with a game of chess, checkers, or **backgammon**. In the cities, people visit friends, shop, or watch television. Children like to play *oonch neech*, a game similar to tag.

backgammon

Did you know?
According to strict religious guidelines, Muslims should not eat pork or anything containing blood. Acceptable food is called *halal*. Anything unacceptable is called haram.

Food in Pakistan is flavorful and sometimes very spicy. Cooks use **herbs** and spices to prepare meat and vegetable dishes. A day in Pakistan begins with a small breakfast of bread, eggs, fruits, and coffee or tea. Curry, a dish that often includes meat and vegetables with rice, is a popular lunch item. For dinner, families gather around a low table, or *takht*. Kebabs, or skewers of grilled meat, are often enjoyed. Families may also make *karahi*, a filling dish of lamb, beef, or chicken cooked in tomato sauce.

karahi

kebabs

Pakistanis celebrate national and religious holidays. On August 14, they celebrate the day in 1947 when Pakistan gained its independence. **Republic** Day takes place on March 23. The streets fill with parades, and people listen to the president give a speech. The president also hands out awards to many Pakistanis.

Most Pakistanis are Muslims. They celebrate Islamic holidays throughout the year. Muharram is the first month of the Islamic calendar, beginning with the Islamic New Year. **Ramadan** is the ninth month of the calendar. During Ramadan, people **fast** during the day. Eid al-Fitr marks the end of Ramadan, and families and friends gather for a large feast.

Islam guides many Pakistanis in their daily lives. Muslims pray five times a day and worship at mosques. The Faisal Mosque in Islamabad is the largest mosque in Pakistan, covering 54,000 square feet (5,000 square meters). Four tall **minarets** rise at its corners.

Muslims come to the Faisal Mosque to listen to teachings from the Qur'an. At the mosque, over 300,000 Pakistanis can worship and pray together. The mosque is a place where Pakistanis unite to honor their religion and celebrate their country.

Fast Facts About Pakistan

Pakistan's Flag

The flag of Pakistan shows a star and crescent moon in white on a green background. On the left side of the flag sits a white rectangle. The crescent moon, the star, and the green color are all symbols of Islam, the official religion of Pakistan. The flag was adopted in 1947.

Official Name: Islamic Republic of Pakistan

Area: 307,374 square miles
(796,095 square kilometers);
Pakistan is the 36th largest country
in the world.

Capital City:	Islamabad
Important Cities:	Karachi, Lahore, Faisalabad, Rawalpindi
Population:	184,404,791 (July 2010)
Official Languages:	Urdu and English
National Holiday:	Republic Day (March 23)
Religions:	Muslim (95%), Other (5%)
Major Industries:	farming, manufacturing, mining, services
Natural Resources:	farmland, coal, oil, limestone, salt, natural gas, iron ore, copper
Manufactured Products:	appliances, cars, carpets, clothing, electronics, chemicals, machinery
Farm Products:	cotton, wheat, rice, sugarcane, fruits, vegetables, dairy products, beef, lamb
Unit of Money:	rupee

Glossary

archaeologists—scientists who study the remains of past civilizations

backgammon—a game of skill and chance played with a board, pieces known as checkers, and dice

dunes—hills of sand

fast—to choose not to eat

habitat—the environment in which a plant or animal usually lives

herbs—plants used in cooking; most herbs are used to add flavor to food.

Kashmir—a region in northern Pakistan; India, Pakistan, and China all claim parts of Kashmir.

minarets—towers next to mosques; people stand in minarets to call Muslims to prayer.

natural resources—materials in the earth that are taken out and used to make products or fuel

Olympics—international games held every two years; the Olympics alternate between summer sports and winter sports.

Ramadan—the ninth month of the Islamic calendar; Ramadan is a time when Muslims fast from sunrise to sunset.

refugees—people who leave one country and go to another because of war or natural disasters

republic—a nation governed by elected leaders instead of a monarch

service jobs—jobs that perform tasks for people or businesses

squash—a game played in an enclosed court with long-handled rackets and a rubber ball; players can hit the rubber ball off any of the walls of the court.

tributaries—streams or rivers that flow into larger streams or rivers

wetlands—wet, spongy land; bogs, marshes, and swamps are wetlands.

To Learn More

AT THE LIBRARY
Crompton, Samuel Willard. *Pakistan*. New York, N.Y.: Chelsea House Publishers, 2007.

DeAngelis, Gina. *Pakistan*. Mankato, Minn.: Blue Earth Books, 2004.

Heinrichs, Ann. *Pakistan*. New York, N.Y.: Children's Press, 2004.

ON THE WEB
Learning more about Pakistan is as easy as 1, 2, 3.

1. Go to www.factsurfer.com.

2. Enter "Pakistan" into the search box.

3. Click the "Surf" button and you will see a list of related Web sites.

With factsurfer.com, finding more information is just a click away.

Index

The images in this book are reproduced through the courtesy of: Hervé Bernard / Photolibrary, front cover; Maisei Raman, front cover (flag), p. 28; Jon Eppard, pp. 4-5; Minden Pictures / Masterfile, p. 6 (small); Henry Wilson, pp. 6-7, 10 (top & middle), 23 (bottom), 29 (bill & coin); John Braid, p. 10 (bottom); Gerard Lacz / Photolibrary, pp. 10-11; AFP / Getty Images, pp. 12, 19 (left); Robert Harding / Photolibrary, p. 14; Bill Stevenson / Photolibrary, p. 15; Andia / Alamy, pp. 16-17; economic images / Alamy, p. 18; Caro / Alamy, p. 19 (right); Getty Images, p. 20; Rolf Bruderer / Photolibrary, p. 21; Martin Wright / Photolibrary, p. 22; Laurence Gough, p. 23 (top); Associated Press, pp. 24, 25, 27 (small); Bruno Morandi / Photolibrary, pp. 26-27.